Arrangements for Ladies' Trio or Ensemble

BY TOM FETTKE

Including *The Birthday of a King,*
a minicantata for ladies' voices.

D1518841

PUBLISHING COMPANY

KANSAS CITY, MO 64141

CONTENTS

A Christmas Prayer 100

A Stable Prayer. 47

Advent Celebration. 65

Canticle of Praise 53

Good News of Great Joy. 4

He Is Worthy of Praise 114

Hear the Angels Shouting 38

How Should a King Come? 17

Hymn of Triumph 82

Lift Up Your Eyes. 62

Lion of Judah 76

Magnificat 93

Mary's Little Boy Chile 26

O Holy Night 34

Prepare Ye the Way 87

Prepare Ye the Way of the Lord. 85

Rejoice with Exceeding Great Joy 107

The Birthday of a King *(minicantata)*. 80

The Birthday of a King *(song)* 101

We Wish You a Merry Christmas. 119

We Would Worship Thee. 32

What Can We Give to the King? 48

You Can Trust God 41

4

Good News of Great Joy

with "Good News, Angels Are a-Singin'"
and "Go, Tell It on the Mountain"

ROBIN WOLAVER
and JULIE ADAMS

BILL WOLAVER
S.S.A. arr. by Tom Fettke

CD: 03

Now the joy-ful song was sung,_____ the years of wait-ing past._____ Em-man-u-el, the hope of earth,_____ was born to us at last. Good news! Good news of great joy!_____ The mar-vel-ous sto-ry un-folds. Good

10

*"Good News, Angels Are a-Singin'"
(Traditional Spiritual, new lyrics by Robin Wolaver)

CD: 05

*"Go Tell It on the Mountain" (Traditional Spiritual)

**Cued notes optional

12

13

14

How Should a King Come?

CAROL OWENS

JIMMY OWENS
Arr. by J. O. and Tom Fettke

1. How should a king come?
2. How should a king come?

(11) *parts optional*

mf

E- ven a child knows the an - swer, of course: In a

parts optional

mf

E- ven a com-mon-er un - der-stands He should

(11)

coach of gold with a pure_____ white horse! In the

come for his trea-sures and his hous - es and lands! He should

(15)

beau - ti - ful cit - y in the prime_____ of the day; And the

dine up - on sum-mer straw - ber - ries and milk, And

(15)

trum - pets should cry and the crowds___ make way! And the

sleep up - on bed - clothes of sat - in and silk! And

flags fly high in the morn - ing sun, And the peo - ple all cheer for the

high on a hill his cas - tle should glow With the lights of the cit - y like

sov - er - eign one! And ev - 'ry - one knows that's the

jew - els be - low! And ev - 'ry - one knows that's the

way that it's done,

way that it's done,

Unison
mp
That's the way that a king should come!

Unison
That's the way that a king should come!

CD: 09 | 1st time
CD: 10 | 2nd time

1st time: repeat
2nd time: go on

How should a king come?

On a star-filled night in-to Beth - le - hem Rode a

wea - ry wo-man and a wor-ried man; And the on - ly sound in the

cob-ble-stone street Was the shuf-fle and the ring of their don - key's feet. And a

King lay hid in a vir-gin's womb, And there were no crowds to

see Him come. At last in a barn in a

man-ger of hay He

24

Mary's Little Boy Chile

J. H.

JESTER HAIRSTON
Arr. by Bill Wolaver
S.S.A. arr. by Tom Fettke

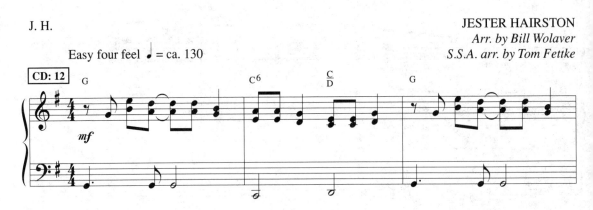

Long time a-go in Beth - le - hem,___ so the Ho - ly Bi - ble say,

28

lit - tle boy chile was born._____ Hark! Now hear the

an - gels sing, "New King is born to-day,_____ And

man will live for - ev - er - more_____ be - cause of Christ - mas day."__

Trum- pets sound and an - gels sing;

31

We Would Worship Thee

J.E.P.

JOE E. PARKS
Arr. by Tom Fettke

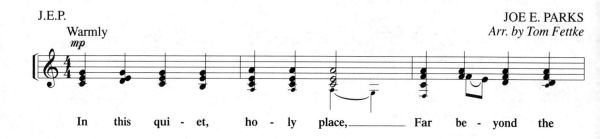

In this qui - et, ho - ly place,_____ Far be - yond the

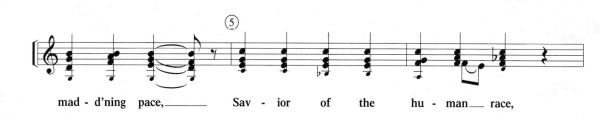

mad - d'ning pace,_____ Sav - ior of the hu - man_ race,

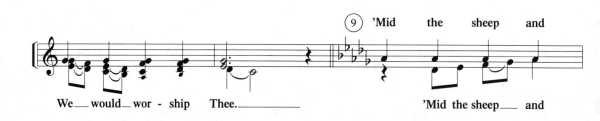

We_ would_ wor - ship Thee._____ 'Mid the sheep_ and

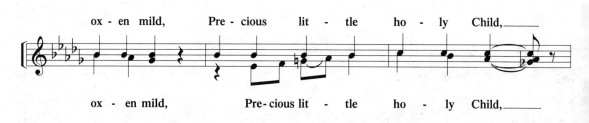

ox - en mild, Pre - cious lit - tle ho - ly Child,_____

ox - en mild, Pre - cious lit - tle ho - ly Child,_____

Son of Mar - y, un - de - filed, We would__ wor - ship

Thee._____ Trib - ute now we hum - bly bring;_____

Songs of___ joy we glad - ly sing. While the bells of

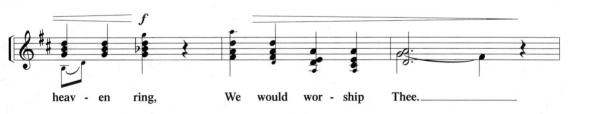

heav - en ring, We would wor - ship Thee._____

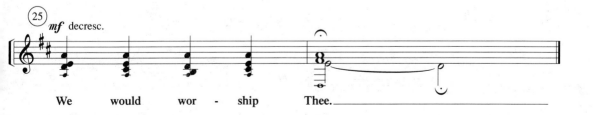

We would wor - ship Thee._____

O Holy Night

A. A.

CD: 15

ADOLPHE ADAM
Arr. by Camp Kirkland and Tom Fettke
S.S.A. arr. by Tom Fettke

Gently ♩ = ca. 69
"O Little Town of Bethlehem" (Redner)

mf

rit.

♩. = ca. 72

Unison ⑦ *mf*

O ho - ly night!___ The

stars are bright-ly shin - ing; It is the night of the dear Sav-ior's

⑬

birth._____ Long lay the world_____ in sin and er - ror

vine,＿＿＿＿＿ O night＿＿＿＿＿＿ when Christ was born! O

29 night,＿＿＿＿＿＿ O ho - ly night, O night di -

CD: 16   **34** _ff_

vine!＿＿＿＿＿ Christ＿＿＿＿＿ is the

_ff_

Lord;＿＿＿＿＿ Oh, praise＿＿＿＿＿ His name for - ev - er! His

_8va_   _8va_   _8va_   _8va_

Hear the Angels Shouting

(Jesus Christ Is Born)

Short Call to Worship

or Concert Opener

DON COLLINS

TOM FETTKE

With great strength ♩ = ca. 120

CD: 17

ho - ly, ho - ly; Glo - ry,

laud; Glo - ry, laud,_____ and praise!_____

8va

You Can Trust God

D. H.

DOUG HOLCK
Arr. by Tom Fettke

1. You can trust God__ to keep His prom-is - es;__ You can

trust God__ to keep His word.   You can trust God__ to keep His

42

prom-is - es;_____ You can trust the Lord___ to keep His word.

⑬ Al - le - lu - ia!_____ Al - le -

lu - ia! Al - le - lu - ia!_____

CD: 19 God will keep His word._____ 2. To___

Solo I (or unison)

44

45

46

CD: 22

God has kept His word.

Al - le - lu - ia! Al - le -

lu - ia! Al - le - lu - ia!

God has kept His word. God has kept His word.

2nd time: left hand only

A Stable Prayer

KEN BIBLE

TOM FETTKE
Arr. by Tom Fettke

What Can We Give to the King?

B. McG. and M. D.

BARRY McGUIRE and MIKE DEASY
Arr. by Tom Fettke

20 F   G   C

Give Him a love   that's ten - der and true,_____ And He'll

Dm7   Em7   FM7   Am/F#   *Unison*

give it   all back____ to you._____   Yes, He'll

24 F/G   G   C   Dm7/C   C   F/E/C   **CD: 24**   *D.S. al Coda*

give it   all back   to you.

CODA F   F/G   G   F/G   C/E   C

mf

Give Him all glo - ry,   His   peo - ple on earth;_____

mf

52

* If the ensemble is composed of 3 singers, two singers should sing Part I and the third voice should be the answer (Part II).
  If the ensemble is more than three, divide the group as evenly as you can.

Canticle of Praise

Arr. by Camp Kirkland and Tom Fettke
S.S.A. arr. by Tom Fettke

54

We sing glo-ri-a to Christ, Je-sus Christ.

CD: 28

*"O Come, All Ye Faithful"
(Trad. carol)

mf

O come, all ye

mf smoother

faith - ful, Joy - ful and tri - um - phant. O

come ye, O come____ ye to Beth - le -

a- dore Him. O come let us a-
a- dore Him. O come, let us a-

dore Him, Christ
dore Him, Christ

the Lord.
the Lord.

CD: 29

58

Christ the Lord,

Christ the Lord! We sing

glo-ri-a, glo-ri-a!

Lift Up Your Eyes

Short Call to Worship
for Advent

LINDA LEE JOHNSON
Based on Isaiah 60
With excitement ♩. = ca. 72

TOM FETTKE

Lift up your eyes____ and see____ the glo - ry of____ the Lord;____ A - rise and

glo - ry of your God.

A - rise, a - rise, rise and

shine!

Advent Celebration

(Medley)

Arr. by Tom Fettke

Smooth and flowing ♩ = ca. 72

With warmth

⑤ *Unison*
mf *"Welcome, Jesus" (Dutch Traditional–T. Fettke)

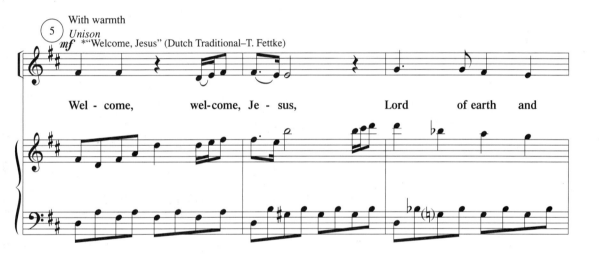

Wel - come,   wel-come, Je - sus,   Lord   of earth   and

⑨

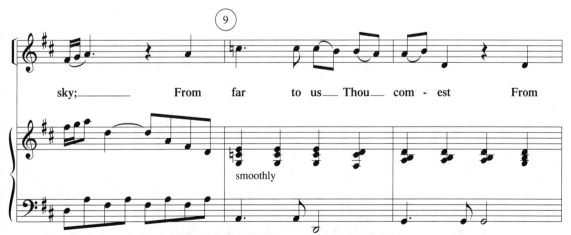

sky;_____ From   far   to us__ Thou__ com - est   From

smoothly

Narrator: For unto us a child is born, unto us a son is given: and the government shall be upon his shoulders.

accel.

CD: 33

"His Name" (Adapt. from Is. 9:6 - Purday)

Emphatically ♩ = ca. 92

mf

His name, shall be called Won - der -

His name, shall be called Won - der -

mf

ful; Won - der - ful;

ful; Won - der - ful;

Ped.

His name shall be called Coun - sel -

His name shall be called Coun - sel -

68

"Blessed Be the Name" (W. H. Clark - R. E. Hudson)

CD: 34

a tempo ♩ = 100

rit.

48 Smooth, but energetic

Unison *mf*

Bless-ed be the name, bless-ed be the name, Bless-ed be the name of the

52 Lord. Bless-ed be the name, bless-ed be the name,

56 *Div.* "At the Name of Jesus" (C. M. Noel - C. Durhan)

Bless-ed be the name of the Lord. At the name of

70

gin - ning   was   the   might - y   Word.

Remain strong

His   name shall   be   the Coun - sel - lor,   the

Remain strong

might - y   Prince   of   Peace;   Of   all   earth's king - doms

CD: 35

Con - quer - or,   whose reign shall nev - er   cease.

72

"O Come, All Ye Faithful" (J. F. Wade, tr. F. Oakely - J. F. Wade)

us a - dore_____ Him,_____

Christ_____ the

Lord._____

Lion of Judah

R. B. and S. M.

RAY BOLTZ and STEVE MILLIKAN
Arr. by Tom Fettke

peo - ple start___ to sing.___ For they would be - hold,___ as
ar - mies at___ His side.___ Could this be the One,___ a

scrip - ture fore - told,___ a might - y King of Kings.___
car - pen - ter's son,___ a man con - demned to die?___

cued notes 2nd verse

But He came as a child,___ not like they___ had
But a Li - on roared___ deep in - side___ this

78

The Birthday of a King
A Minicantata for Ladies' Voices

"Hymn of Triumph"

NARRATOR 1   Every valley shall be exalted, and every mountain and hill shall be made low: and the crooked shall be made straight, and the rough places plain.

*NARRATOR 2   And the glory of the Lord shall be revealed, and all flesh shall see it together: for the mouth of the Lord hath spoken it.

NARRATOR 3   Arise, shine, for thy light is come, and the glory of the Lord is risen upon thee.
(Start music)
(Isaiah 40:4-5; 60:1, KJV)

"Prepare Ye the Way of the Lord"

NARRATOR 1   For unto us a child is born, unto us a son is given: and the government shall be upon his shoulder: and his name shall be called *(Start music)*

NARRATOR 2   Wonderful, Counselor, The mighty God,
NARRATOR 3   The everlasting Father, The Prince of Peace.
(Isaiah 9:6, KJV)

"Magnificat"

"A Christmas Prayer" (OPTIONAL)

NARRATOR 1   And there were shepherds living out in the fields nearby, keeping watch over their flocks at night.

NARRATOR 2   An angel of the Lord appeared to them, and the glory of the Lord shone around them, and they were terrified.

NARRATOR 3   But the angel said to them, "Do not be afraid. I bring you good news of great joy that will be for all the people. *(Start music)*

---

*(One person may do the narrative throughout, if desired.)

NARRATOR 1 (or all):   "Today in the town of David a Savior has been born to you; he is Christ the Lord. This will be a sign to you: You will find a baby wrapped in strips of cloth and lying in a manger."
(Luke 2:8-12, NIV)

"The Birthday of a King"

NARRATOR 1   [Herod] sent [the wise men] to Bethlehem, saying, "Go and search diligently for the child, and when you have found him bring me word, that I too may come and worship him."

NARRATOR 2   When they had heard the king they went their way; and lo, the star which they had seen in the East went before them, till it came to rest over the place where the child was.

NARRATOR 3   When they saw the star, they rejoiced exceedingly with great joy; *(Start music)* and going into the house they saw the child with Mary his mother, and they fell down and worshiped him.
(Matthew 2:8-11, RSV)

"Rejoice with Exceeding Great Joy"

NARRATOR 1   The Word became flesh and made his dwelling among us. We have seen his glory, the glory of the One and Only, who came from the Father, full of grace and truth.

NARRATOR 2   For God so loved the world that he gave his one and only Son, that whoever believes in him shall not perish but have eternal life.
(Start music)

NARRATOR 3   For God did not send his Son into the world to condemn the world, but to save the world through him.
(John 1:14; 3:16-17, NIV)

"He Is Worthy of Praise"

"We Wish You a Merry Christmas" *(OPTIONAL)*

Hymn of Triumph

Short Call to Worship,
Service Closer or Concert Opener

LINDA LEE JOHNSON

LUDWIG VAN BEETHOVEN
Arr. by Tom Fettke

hearts are lift - ed, Joined in won - der love, and praise.

Al - le - lu - ia! Al - le - lu - ia! Al - le - lu -

ia!

Prepare Ye the Way of the Lord

Adapted from Isaiah 40:3, 4 by W. D. Y.

WILLIAM DAVID YOUNG
Arr. by Tom Fettke

Prepare Ye The Way

KARLA WORLEY

DAVID MADDUX
Arr. by Doug Holck
S. S. A. arr. by Tom Fettke

Pre - pare ye the way of the Lord,

make straight a path for Him;

88

know That the glo - ry of ___ the Lord has been ___ re -

vealed ___ By the lives ___ that are ___ re -

deemed and the hearts that are healed. ___ So

Unison

mf

lift up your hearts and look for the Lord; Our prais - es draw Him

near. He is read-y to come; pre-

pare the way for Him here.

Lord has been re-vealed By the

CD: 44

Div.

The glo-ry of the

Magnificat

LINDA LEE JOHNSON

TOM FETTKE

94

soul _____ bless - es _____ my _____ God and Cre -

a - tor. _____ My spir - it re - joic - es in

God, my Sav - ior; My soul

accel. | CD: 46 | *mf*

mag - ni - fies the Lord. _____ For the

accel.

95

96

a - tor._____ My spir - it re -

joic - es in God, my Sav - ior; My soul

mag - ni - fies the Lord._____

CD: 49

Ho - ly, ho - ly,

A Christmas Prayer

Response

PHILLIPS BROOKS

TOM FETTKE

O ho - ly Child of Beth - le - hem,

De - scend to us_____ we pray.

Cast out our sin,_____ and en - ter in; Be

born_____ in us_____ to - day. A - men.

The Birthday of a King

W. H. N.

W. H. NEIDLINGER
Arr. by Tom Fettke

sky was bright with a ho - ly light O'er the place where Je - sus

lay. Al - le - lu - ia!_____ Oh, how the

an - gels sang! Al - le - lu - ia! How it

rang! And the sky_____ was bright with a

104

CODA

Stronger

(38) Listesso Maestoso ♩ = ♩.

Div.

King. Al - le - lu - ia!_____ Oh, how the

an - gels sang! Al - le - lu - ia!_____ How it

(42)

rang! And the sky_____ was bright with a

106

ho - ly light; 'Twas the birth - day of a

Sav - ior. Al - le - lu - ia! Al - le -

lu - ia! 'Twas the birth - day

of a King.

Rejoice with Exceeding Great Joy

L. W.

LANNY WOLFE
Arr. by Tom Fettke

110

111

when they saw the star,____ they re - joiced with great joy!____

When they saw the star,____ they re - joiced with great joy!____

When they saw the star,____ they re - joiced with great joy!____ They re -

He Is Worthy of Praise

D. H.

DOUG HOLCK
S.S.A. arr. by Tom Fettke

118

We Wish You a Merry Christmas

TRADITIONAL
Spirited

TRADITIONAL ENGLISH TUNE
Arr. by Tom Fettke